CITY NOISE

by Karla Kuskin · illustrated by Renée Flower

HarperCollins Publishers

For Maddie and Jake, the new noisemakers
—K. K.

In memory of my mother,
whose love still shelters her little wren
—R. F.

So what did you see?

**An old tin can,
It was sitting in the gutter
I took it in my hand.**

**I held it very carefully against my ear
And listened, listened, listened.**

So what did you hear?

**Squalling
Calling**

Crashing
Rushing

**Honking
Joking**

**Belching
Smoking**

Buying
Selling

Laughing
Yelling

Running
Wheeling

**Roaring
Squealing**

Cars and garbage

Reds and greens

Girls and women

Men

Machines

Getting
Giving

Dogs and boys

Living

Living

Living

City noise.

Library of Congress Cataloging-in-Publication Data Kuskin, Karla. City Noise / by Karla Kuskin;

illustrated by Renée Flower. p. cm.   Summary: In this poem, an old tin can becomes an urban

conch shell when, held against a child's ear, it reveals the sounds of a bustling city. ISBN 0-06-021076-1.

—ISBN 0-06-021077-X (lib. bdg.) 1. City and town life—Juvenile poetry.   2. Children's poetry, American.

[1. City and town life—Poetry. 2. Sound—Poetry. 3. Noise—Poetry. 4. American Poetry.]

I. Flower, Renée, ill. II. Title. PS3561.U79C57 1994 91-44213 811'.54—dc20

CIP AC 1 2 3 4 5 6 7 8 9 10 ❖ First Edition